The Boatman of Murshidabad

The Boatman of Murshidabad

•*Selected Poems*•

MADHU KAILAS

ALEPH

ALEPH

ALEPH BOOK COMPANY
An independent publishing firm
promoted by *Rupa Publications India*

First published in India in 2021 by
Aleph Book Company
7/16 Ansari Road, Daryaganj
New Delhi 110002

Copyright © Kingshuk Basu 2021

The author has asserted his moral rights.

All rights reserved.

The views and opinions expressed in this book are those of the author and the publisher is in no way liable for the same.

No part of this publication may be reproduced, transmitted, or stored in a retrieval system, in any form or by any means, without permission in writing from Aleph Book Company.

ISBN: 978-93-90652-82-2

1 3 5 7 9 10 8 6 4 2

Printed at Parksons Graphics Pvt. Ltd, Mumbai

This book is sold subject to the condition that it shall not, by way of trade or otherwise, be lent, resold, hired out, or otherwise circulated without the publisher's prior consent in any form of binding or cover other than that in which it is published.

To my family

CONTENTS

On Poetry	xi
1. The Day a Song Dared to Soar	1
2. Copper Mine	3
3. Moths of N. Marshall Street	5
4. Music of Our Species	8
5. Vibrations	10
6. Notes on Drought	12
7. Transparent Men	14
8. Fishing Village	16
9. Shakuntala's Plea	18
10. The Parrot's Theatre	21
11. Temple Tourists	23
12. Darjeeling	25
13. Born Again as a Cherry Tree	28
14. Love Grows	30

15. Statue's Poem	34
16. The Boatman of Murshidabad	36
17. You Leave for the Mountains	39
18. Wait	41
19. Voice of the Hills	43
20. Seagulls	45
21. Thaw	46
22. Poetry for Tomorrow	47
23. After the Rains	49
24. Flow	50
25. How Strong You Had to Be—From a Miner's Son	52
26. Birth of a Myriad Waterfalls	55
27. The Forest Sings	57
28. Silence of Butterflies	59
29. To Love Myself	60
30. Sidewalk Cafe	62
31. Back from Work	64
32. Blue Boat	66
33. Some Nights	68
34. I Come for Myself	69
35. Monsoon Evening	71
36. Azure Soul	72

37. Inheritance of Shame	73
38. Train Journey	75
39. Strange Times	78
40. Dance with Ancestors	80
41. African Sun	81
42. Sea of Tears	83
43. Winter's Prayer	84
44. Purple Cord	87
45. Later On	88
46. My Joys	90
47. Keys Made of Sunshine	92
48. Shadows Are Born Out of Light	93
49. A Plant, A Leaf, A Leaf of a Plant, and I	95
50. The Flute Player	97
Acknowledgements	99
Index of First Lines	102
About The Poet	105

ON POETRY

My poetry was not planned. My poetry was not deliberated upon. It was an accident couple of decades back. After years of my devotion to my craft and our mutual evolution, even today, poetry adamantly maintains a relationship of the 'undefined and unknown'. A relationship that has no boundaries and norms, and offers no understanding and gratification of permanence. For me, poetry resides both at the fringes and at the core of my existence. And, it is all encompassing but inaccessible. Each poem is a revelation that points me toward an awareness that is larger than me. It is through this writing process that I discover, I think about, I access, and I feel the world in its full richness.

The best way of trying to describe the act of writing a poem is 'surrendering to a flow' that originates in a larger, universal consciousness—its origin, cadence, and manifestation are beyond my control. It is not that I am possessed by some unnatural force, or I don't deliberate on the tools of the art, but essentially what the poem wants to express belongs to the poem and is marginally mine. This is where the creative tension tears me and my writing apart; this is how a poem is born and how it grows. To add to this complexity of 'unbelonging', individual 'words' (which, of course, are central to this art form) actually constrain the poem with their inadequacies. I therefore spend considerable time on finding the right 'word' or more specifically on the 'halo surrounding the word', which is its potential of manifesting the intangible and inexpressible elements of human emotions.

To me, poetry is an integral part of living; not just in terms of the interactions and the interconnectedness of the various elements of our lives, but because I can sense it is always breathing alongside me whether I am actively engaged with it or not. I have never been able to 'plan a poem'. At best, I write a couple of lines and then the formation of a poem itself takes over. It navigates and delves into areas seemingly disjoint and throws up a fantastic pattern of assimilation of many dimensions. It is as a result of this sort of creative process that I have come to look at a poem as not only the existential testimony of a poet's engagement with the art and creative liberation, but also as an entity that has a life of its own before and after the event not just in terms of the relationship between the writer and the reader, but more significantly in an absolute manner as a timeless expression of human existence.

I am not formally trained in the art of poetry. However, I find that as a result of this, I am able to experiment with the form, especially when it comes to crafting free verse—I am able to range far and wide in a way that might not have been possible had I been rigorously schooled in this art form. My poems have helped me look at this world and our humanness in unexpected ways. To me, poetry is empathetic, joyous, and liberating. It is my hope that readers will find in them new ways of looking at and experiencing the boundless wonders of our existence.

THE DAY A SONG DARED TO SOAR

The day the travellers returned
and picked new faces for rebirth,

we stopped meeting in the dark
where we had to compress ourselves
into eyes and dissolve the rest.

Eyes that packed our souls into fragments
for easy passage through silence,

from my breath to yours
with such intensity that we could only be us
not seen, not heard, not touched.

We were not sensed
in the dark of invisible flames
only we knew about
and we carried the faith between our eyes.

Like one touch of your finger could burst open life,
we cracked open the day to produce daylight—

the day we let mammoth weight shed itself
and bright light worked on building our limbs,
infusing blood in tired skin,

the day we held each other in our arms.
The day a song dared to soar,
longed to be more,
and scratched the surface of joy.

COPPER MINE

Hollowed earth—
a large reservoir of emptiness.
Deep down where only
the moon can touch
dregs of an empty cup,
static turquoise fluid
of residual copper blood.

Cyclopean machines
crawl like dwarf ants
along grooves etched by mortal hands.
Gnaw at rocks
startled out of deep sleep
to be stripped.

An ancient cave painting
tumbles out of extinction
delineated by insect blood
on ochre flats.

Dead insects scrabble out of rocks
on the landscape of our civilization.

MOTHS OF N. MARSHALL STREET

In an apartment
older than a century.
Still young
with eyes that are newborn
seeking, not seeing yet.
My airy steps
timid of thresholds then,
still remain ambushed
by the velvet moths
of N. Marshall Street.

Bricks thick with paint.
White over red,
and red over white,
to keep the rhyme
interspaced by vine.
Walls hoary and pensive,
weighed down by the chill
slanting in

from Lake Michigan
a few blocks away.
They sang sweetly
in the night—
insect hushes and inaudible jazz.

They had all come
to rest in the dark
and in bizarre silence.
I saw studio walls
studded with throbbing stars,
countless velvet hearts
moistly perched
in random grey.
This brightest scene,
in a moment-split
filled my inside
once, forever.

I, with moth sorcery,
plucked them daintily—
careful not to hurt us.

One by one
wings quivered and
left into the dusk.
With my walls bared,
and windows facing the dark,
we watched the sun set
till the end.

In summer in Milwaukee—
first, the sun loiters;
then, it lingers and lingers
to a point of numbness.
Wreathes the crown
of city hall's bell tower
with lavish crimson light.
Till you give in,
and sleep takes you
helpless.
Then, what happens to the sun
and to the moths
are outside your sleep.

MUSIC OF OUR SPECIES

Open skies pouring stars...
and we stretch it with brittle hands
to cover the sharp edges of our ocean.

Our sweeping ecstasy and grief
collected in crucibles with the passage of time.
My blood touches your joy. Your eyes sing my truth.
Our music illuminate chambers of our heart—
red and non-verbal.

On shores far apart...
in search of a language that will live us,
again, together in love. We sing
for our discovery and rebirth.

So much is folded in
that silence is more eloquent than arranging words.
With music we walk towards us.

When we meet, we stop and listen to us humming.
A blue orb abuzz; recedes into a hum.
Grows faint, and recedes...
grows fainter, and recedes further...
to minute vibrations of our rhythm.

Our music falls silent in the arms of stars.

VIBRATIONS

You are so quiet I can almost listen to *you beating*.
All these years I never felt you as vibrations.
You have been like spring,
like the elegance of movement,
like a melody, a companion, a lover;

you have been so many things—
that were born to the senses,
lived in emotions,
external to me.

Now vibrations
that can fill me up if only I can cease to be.
We are changing; I am trying.

There is nothing surreal about you. Like me,
you are still flesh and bones, and we have not given up
our existence in this universe.

We see ourselves; we speak alone and we have learnt
to smile at ourselves.

You are so joyful—I can see you waving at me.
Down a path to new places
where you cannot leave me behind
and you cannot take me along with you.

You are so quiet—I am listening hard.
Sorrows and shadows are sloughed off.
There is no place for tears and regrets.
No hurts.

We are growing back into children; not new lovers.
You are so joyful—I break into a smile.
We are laughing together
and nothing else.

NOTES ON DROUGHT

The earth nibbles on traces of desiccated grass and
   polishes itself.
Then it cracks open to find nourishment. The edges curl
   inward
like burnt paper in half-existence.

The animals stand still and gaze hard into the nucleus of
   numb haze.
They transform into decorative skulls with frail edges
of eye sockets and nostrils, still sniffing for rain.

Dry clouds rumble into brains like drumbeats for the
   dead.
The vultures are too sapped to circle overhead.
Meanwhile, in the villages farmers kill themselves.

The coops are empty. No one knows where the birds
   went.

Some say they were snatched mid-air to fatten the dearth.

Ancestors awake in their memories, deep in anguish.
They sense it's time to shed ribs, and cauterise the flesh
to preserve dry seeds.

Earth gives up last straws of grain apparition to dust.
The waiting gets sharper with each blast.
Air rises through the bones to scorch and
collect moisture from the marrow to prepare bone-dust.

TRANSPARENT MEN

Once a man
braved to walk through the sun.
Thereafter, he cast no shadows,
and colours could choose him no more.

His sight was usurped by the keepers of light,
who threatened to purge him
into nothingness
and less.

Some whispered in spite
that he drank darkness from light,
and spun threads of silence
that trapped minds.

His beloved met him on his return
in the open, bathed by liquid sun.
She asked, 'Tell me: how is it there?'
And he said, 'I wish I had words to limn

how beautiful they are, those transparent men!'

'And love?' she implored.
He drew her close and said,
'Love, they know nothing of.
It is only on this side of the sun
we find love to see ourselves.'

Happily, she held his hand,
and recounted when she was a child,
she had a glass doll
through whom she could see it all.

FISHING VILLAGE

In a small village, by the sea,
smaller than a sienna dot
on a silver-washed-shore forehead.
Where all the people
are drunk on gale and sated with sand

hold hands like an invisible net
of trust and nylon-grit.
They walk out into the sea
to catch the infant horizon-sun
very, very far away.

So far away that I have never been,
I will never be at their water-dance
and feast of fish songs and fish memories,
and I will not know how they love
their mermaids on ocean beds.

Basted in salt and sweat
skin ripens into leather,
and leather cuts into grooves
like time-prints on sand
and cloud-trails etched in wary eyes.

White cliffs sculpted as epithets
of all the people who sail their lives
in vessels of faith—
like chunks of gold, like powdered suns,
on capricious sea breasts

where fears drown in green waves
and laughter rides their crests
in a heady froth—
there night comes to rest
with requiems for the dead.

SHAKUNTALA'S PLEA

Beyond remembrance, you are so distant,
consumed by royal duties
and jewelled might.
You have turned ancient and your justice too.

Remnants of your shadows.
Myth of your presence.
Your voice, embracing an oath
and lending hope, has shrivelled in our hearts.

You loom poignantly over us, our stories.
We lament your amnesia. The luxury of it!
O Dushyanta! When will you remember?

Our fateful love, deeper than the forest,
older than time, greener than bird songs
and nature's mating cries.

Lost in the wilderness,
on the banks of the Malini, in the foothills of the
 Shivaliks,
our love seeks an insignia to stay alive.

Like a thunderclap at the tip of your arrow—
I blossomed in the writhing of an injured deer.
Yielded to your pursuit of sailing pleasures.

Dushyanta, do you know, it still bleeds?
From numerous wounds spawned
by the primordial one. Inflicted by you
the deer forgot to die.
So, we live thirsty and rabid.

And I? In my mindless pleasure
of contemplating our love,
I earned Durvasa's curse!

The fish with an appetite for a billion people's dreams,
has swallowed us, and kept it secret
for thousands of years!

Thus, we live estranged, forgotten.
We wait for our fisherman.

Dushyanta, it is not for my bereaved heart,
or for our union, is my plea.
The story promises us—
you were to return and find a young boy, Bharata,
prying open a lion's mouth and counting its teeth.

THE PARROT'S THEATRE

Our explorer friends
chanced upon a floating orb
inhabited by monkeys and apes.

On docking, they exclaimed,
'My goodness, what a mess
they have made of this place!'

A parrot perched in the greens
snapped in nonchalant bliss,
'My goodness, what a mess!'

The monkeys screeched in glee.
In endless frolic and screech
they lapped up the parrot's jest.

Seeing the explorers troubled
the leader made a stern comment,
'It's all the parrot's fault!'

The parrot perched in the greens
snapped in nonchalant bliss,
'It's all the parrot's doing! Wring its neck.'

The monkeys broke out in wild applause.
Started chanting the parrot's praise.
Their leader donned a sagacious face.

Our explorer friends left in haste.
In baffled awe they said,
'They have figured it out. We do not understand.'

TEMPLE TOURISTS

The rock has a womb of faith,
carries an ancient temple.
We are tourist-ants crawling with astonished eyes.

The colossal walls rise in stark rectitude,
and conjoin earth and the sky.
The body is chiselled and painted with mythology.

This ensemble of our million deities—
I tell our sons—this is our story,
delicacy of stone in three dimensions.

I look up at a blue rectangle splashed with sun,
in its cradle a giant stone elephant
in full splendour with demolished tusks.

It is cut in slabs steeply stacked upward;
I wonder why we climb to still our mind.
She looks back to find I have been left behind.

In cold stone chambers where the monks lived,
I squeeze in with the boys and pretend to pray.
A life-size tunnel bored into the rock.

At the temple door the breeze is cool.
We all are at home; few homeless people
sleep on the cold stone floor.

DARJEELING

I hear your demure flute
play through you, around you
in chiffon lightness
trace your undulations
levitate in your bosom
like a settling soul
float across your valleys
in a string of pearly notes.
Now sad, now joyous
through many births—
your divine music plays on,
endless, endless, endless!

I hear your demure flute
caress hamlets asleep
swaddled in your green peace.
Pulsating lights in the night
like fireflies loving your body
with silver-speck sighs.

The innocence of beautiful lives
born of tea leaves.
Pine trees rise on their toes
to kiss the closed eyes of the sky.
Now I lean in to kiss your forehead
and hold you near.
The velvet aroma of your skin
and your melancholy dreams
play your divine music
(from peak to peak)
endless, endless, endless!

O Darjeeling!
O mountains of my dreams!
How you come alive in me
how you fill me
with your mountain bodies
how I brim over
with your mountain notes.
How I long
to come alive in you,

Madhu Kailas

to be born as a tea leaf
held softly between your lips.

BORN AGAIN AS A CHERRY TREE

I kneel down and bend forward awkwardly
to say new prayers

of finding lost things. I reconstruct old pleas,
litanies of an aged frame

in twisted pain, and porous bones
breathe lightness into gravity.

Forgive me, for ages I looked outward
for meaningful things to come.

Forgive me, I cannot reach you
long after the celebrations have begun.

Forgive me, I cry over things
that are not real.

The sun is real, its golden rays and warmth are real.
Music in the grain of wood is real.

Your hiatus is a universe, and my anguish is real.
My prayers come alive and you are born again

as a cherry tree. You have
infinite pink flowers printed all over your lovely body.

LOVE GROWS
(To: MB)

Love grows
in bougainvillea chaparral
weighing down the fence,
wind chimes dripping time
in honey pots
on the porch, and
enfolding this old house
held together
by the framed sentiments
of a young couple
sworn into new love
oblivious of how love grows
between living walls
that run patiently parallel to life
and meet at crossroads,
battered by rain,
leavened by seasons.

Madhu Kailas

Love grows
at times
in a greenish coat of mould,
in the red bites of termites,
trapped in mothballs
of domestic salt and vinegar.
In silences
and in spite of dark contempt
with gritting teeth,
still love grows
in richness and depth.

So, love grows
in the dimming of our eyes
behind cataract lace,
grey wisps curious
about new born wrinkles
charting the face.

In the blackening of kitchen pots
and sediments
settling in grains

to a hardened crust
for love to test its appetite
and fill the spaces
we solve
inside, and also
in the backyard
in the corner, love listens
from a jilted, three-legged chair
next to a junk lawnmower
occasional jazz
drifting through the window panes
flickering with candlelight
alive in cold glass
like floating lanterns in the night
of Oriental dreams.

And, love grows
with the clinks of your bracelets,
sprinkles of footsteps,
the circular paste marks
in the mirror's corner
left by a medley of bindis

ever kissing your forehead.
In the yellowing, tattered pages
of prayer books
next to blackened
bronze lamps and
an incense stand.

Love grows
through infants and toddlers,
soon teenagers.
Now early to bed
for school in the morning
eagerly dreaming:
Happy Birthday Mom!
Through the years, on this eve,
you will cry a wee bit
as love grows
another year passes.
The years go by.

STATUE'S POEM

Lips chiselled into an enduring smile,
It can no longer cry
except in dreams
when the statue sleeps
ravaged by butterflies.

You chip, you carve, you go deeper.
It is stone compressed with sorrow,
time-locked lips
speaking history's surface
and stone-memories.

Stripped of all tears, nothing to give—the statue smiles.
Immobile, its gaze fixed, the statue smiles—at nothing.

Now, one day, a poem steps out steeped in joy
from a musty, ancient, mummy chest
Finds itself born without limbs, without wings

to go in search of love syllables.
Static and wanting, the poem dies.

Nibbling the dead poem—the statue smiles.

THE BOATMAN OF MURSHIDABAD

The boat holds still its inverted self
drawn out in a mercury leaf turning away from the sun
and seeking the glowing ripples of river-skin.

Where the bamboo oars pierce the water,
as if dealt with invisible resistance they break sharply
and swim away in zebra stripes.

Silver and sea green circles hold the oars motionless,
and arrest my listless eyes
drenched in cool morning breath.

The sun in the vicinity is betrayed by its red streaks
and warming of the chill. The thatched half-dome
is burnished into the boat's crown.

Inside, it's still dark,
but the hanging lantern at the prow
has turned sallow, and burns fruitless.

It's not true that the boatman always sings and rows
 merrily.
At times he sleeps with his torpor
locked in his aching chest, and the moon mourns alone.

His mouth is filled with sand and shrubs
of yesterday's river banks. There are boulders and pebbles
gnawed to silt—they build distant shores.

In the pitch of night, made darker and blind by hunt of
 gore,
through pungent mist, and metal-sharp, the boatman
 ferried us
to a new dawn, marked by crying babies silenced in fright.

Open mouths and tears-in-pause haunt even today.
An egret at the tip of the boat glued like an ensign
catches an imperceptible roll. Aloof and aware in
 harmony.

The day enters the thatched dome
to look for the embers and ashes of the boatman
sleeping in peace on shifting, flowing borders.

YOU LEAVE FOR THE MOUNTAINS

You leave for the mountains
and step into the clouds.
White clouds cover you softly
and you transform into a little girl.

Now you belong to the mist
and settle on the far side
from where only echoes travel back—
one more time an ancient messenger arrives.

I struggle to decipher what seems so simple,
I am back at the start of a journey
betrayed by language,
you have left for the mountains.

Meanwhile, there are scattered hamlets.
There are gardens, white fences, porches,
and large glass panes divide the night into cubes.
There are people and homes and warm fires

and silence surrounds them.
There are two nights at two different points—
they are awake and separate.
Tonight, the snow is fresh and delicate.

The cranes stretch their necks to caress moonlight.
The flames glow along your limbs
and light up your lovely face
somewhere far, far away in the mountains.

WAIT

A deserted station and a long wait.
Here, there is no arrival, no departure—people forget.

No one leaves, people wait, time is elastic,
it stretches through many dimensions and the five senses.

We are a curled-up street dog
and two sparrows stunned by the heat.

All sit with empty resolve.
Shadows shift over red dust with eerie silence

from one end of the planet to the other.
Crisp shapes, then dissolution, dragged across the sky.

Shadows take nothing with them. They were born
without arms and only in two dimensions.

Corrugated tin roof forgets the moon that rose high
above a gulmohar tree, and printed on its body

silver and ash leaves. It was only last night
that the flames turned silver white,

and I felt your lips envelope my sleep.
Now it's all forgotten; now ablaze again.

I stand in the searing heat of gulmohar memories
and watch a yajna created by red earth.

We are all returning to it, after a long wait.
A curled-up dog and two stunned sparrows.

VOICE OF THE HILLS

Now the hills call (again), rising into the sky
laced with crimson and ink blue sashes.
Bodies blossom in the soft earth, thirsting to burst,
yearn for the stars, new and gallant.

A lava heart, so gentle and tame,
in the arms of the evening slipping along its curves,
tender cupped palms hold the day's song
of birds, and the courtship of bees and flowers.

Spent petals are strewn on lichen—only a day to burn
their wanton colours—their brazen lips, deathly and fresh
kiss stones warped in deathless silence.
On the forest floor, in care of the hills, their stories are
    told.

I listen to the distance, always lost in mist and receding,
like a cruel strain of nostalgia on an unending path.

It does not arrive. It does not speak. I pluck a star and plant it in the hills' heart. A lone refuge flickers.

SEAGULLS

The glistening blade of the ocean
where the horizon dares to meet,
at that far edge—the heaven and earth
are cleaved asunder, and fall free into eternity.

Flattened by our myopia—
seagulls rise in new perspectives,
and create random strands of joy
barely traced in the void. Here, there is no fear—

they come near, entrusting their warm bodies
to another species. I surrender to
their white and grey feathers,
and secrets of their flight prints.

I open my body to the winds—
in little pieces,
the salt and the sand
carry me away.

THAW

Long shadows in the snow.
Longer tracks, fresh near and frayed afar,
thin into nowhere. Carrying silence.

The wait for the return of those
who went before is long,
longer than the time it takes to melt it all.

Still, it freezes over to steel water
in helpless inertia
when all I want is the magic of thaw.

To meditate on the release of warmth,
feel the tenderness of wet earth.
To give and be absorbed, losing all form.

POETRY FOR TOMORROW

Yesterday is reduced to a midget box
in the calendar (on the wall).

Tastes like an ashtray,
hemmed by salt lines of dried summer sweat.

Yesterday now belongs to the dead
or the dead parts of the living; but look:

How greedily tomorrow feeds off it,
because tomorrow is growing.

Growing through the night, and
there is still time to choose to feed it right.

The most beautiful pair of eyes belong to 'Daybreak'.
Wide, warm, and tender. They never lie.

Tomorrow I want to look into those eyes
and find new poetry. Free from ashes and midget boxes.

AFTER THE RAINS

A thin layer—sparkle of glass,
a wash of mindfulness.
A liquid membrane projects
delicately into space
this world rebounding
from its hyaloid skin.

After the rains,
energy—new and sublime.
A face tilted forward with lowered eyes,
imagination behind a parasol.
Cautious, dainty steps
frail ankles—wet and glistening.

A hand like marble
extends in a deliberate fashion,
balancing the blue air
and silver light
scent of wet earth—
lush and hungry.

FLOW
(To: MB)

A sweep of your eyelashes
and like the mysterious life of
an invisible wellspring—
twenty years flow.

Remains hint at what we have consumed
and what we have forgotten.
We create static and luminous voids
with reflections that cannot rescue the past.

In search of where we belong
we stick coloured gems and silver deco.
A random pattern is eloquent too,
like how we and our breath blend.

I have held your hands of soft white petals,
over twenty years,

dry wrinkles and blue veins
have grown into my keeping.

I touch your chin
anxious that we do not crumble and become bone dust.
Your smile is not just the language of your lips,
it is how you are built into my soul.

It tells me we are living,
and we still sense for love.
Music plays
to give company and rhythm to our flow.

HOW STRONG YOU HAD TO BE—FROM A MINER'S SON
(To: ARB)

How strong you were, now I know
you had to be, to put bread on our table.
Every day to leave light and air
and enter the belly of darkness. You shuttled
in a wire cage between life and beyond.

You guided your company of live bones and flesh
through residences of the dead.
You walked miles in a strange dimness,
threading bravely through an intricate maze
and tasted the underside of earth's skin.

In the midst of secret streams, the language
of rocks and dead trees, pockets of gas,
sound of metal on rock, the distant blasts
and rumble of coal cars on rails,
you had to be strong.

Madhu Kailas

You heard your breath whisper between thick coal walls,
to find cracks in blocks of pitch dark
your eyes pushed against monstrous weight
to keep the seasons alive for all your men,
you had to be strong.

I strained to hear the metal rims of your boots
return through the night. How proud I was
you could walk through anything.
I just did not know
how strong you had to be.

The heavy battery strapped to your hips
the conical beam of light that swayed ahead of you
streaming from your forehead, I loved so much.
More than just a man, I was proud of
this man embedded with steel and light.

I just did not know how strong you had to be
to put bread on our table. When you returned
I only saw your eyes and your smile.

Later, when I was asleep, the night restored you
from coal dust like magic.

Now you look a shadow,
Those eyes and that smile have dimmed,
you wait to follow.
There is an earthy home you know, I don't.
Now I know, I just know, for forty years.

How strong you were, you had to be
to put bread on our table.

BIRTH OF A MYRIAD WATERFALLS

Longing arrives
with fangs piercing deep and sharp.
The monsoon takes the earth in ardent passion,
thirst blazing in wetness.

I feel ravaged, I shake in disbelief,
I open curtains to such vivid wilderness;
everywhere your eyes
in misty veil over intense green.

Longing returns
from unfelt territory—I have not been.
I ache for this life I will not meet—
everywhere your emptiness.

Like a sprightly fawn
you flow over rounded hilltops—
birth of a myriad waterfalls,
unabashed display of your fertility.

Longing reminds—
music of rain touching nerve ends,
clouds settling on trembling space,
a twilight glow spreading over your frame.

Halfway to heaven
I travel with closed eyes,
rising in the clouds—
everywhere your intimacy—far, far away.

THE FOREST SINGS

The forest has a song that plays
to the two of us in different ages.
I step into the vibration
where I can listen to you listening.

You see the bark peeling off
in silver scars. I enter the ground
to become a tree.
I walk into the sparkling stream

to get closer to your reflection.
You ripple away,
we never exist for each other
save when the forest sings.

The breeze does not carry
the same cadence twice.
It preserves an arrangement of
leaves and flowers in a secret language.

Streaming sun-rays like twining strings
make music—form a conduit
for the heavens to touch us.
When it goes missing

is when we begin to merge,
we drink our cup of darkness
and become one
across boundaries, through the lives of trees

we become one again,
as the forest sings
in surreal despair
imploring us to live, become immortal.

SILENCE OF BUTTERFLIES

Butterflies descend. Twin yellow leaves float;
sea of sunshine. Golden silk strands, maiden's dishevelled
    hair
cascade on to the green forest floor.

Trees. A giant and porous canopy of dreams.
Flowers push back sleepless night. Morning warms
their nub, young petals gather softness and part.

Silence of creation. It puts its lips to the edges;
at the centre. Yellow wings slowly open.
Slowly close. Outside, morning breaks as routine.

TO LOVE MYSELF

Mother, you sent me into this world
with two fists pushing through the earth,
seeking life. Slender saplings, holding up the sky.

Fistful of blue and fine grains
covered my limbs—
the forming of heaven still to come.

You gave me strength to dig into the soil
with naked hands, and distil moisture to make tears.
Claws would sharpen, clog, and break over time.

Mother, you forgot to tell me:
to love myself, here on this earth, in this beautiful life,
alongside seasons and among lovers.

Paper moons drained off all blood,
gave every drop to return me to myself.
Mother, I am not bitter.

Now I blow the conch facing east
before the birth of first light and wonder—
what if you had blessed me to love myself?

Would it be different?
It rains fine through the early days
and soaks everything.

Afterwards, a peacock spreads its august feathers
into the backrest of a throne decked with azure eyes.
It stands tall.

SIDEWALK CAFE

I wait for you
while the sun seeps out of tea bags
against a backdrop of overnight porcelain
retrieved from cold memories.

On the cobblestones, patterned iron dazzles white.
They sit with prim backs, like austere monks
in deep contemplation of laced tablecloths
switched out of yesterday's stains.

I wait for myself as much
to arrive as a mendicant at your soul.
I tilt a hat, or I pull an overcoat
tightly across my chest, shuffling.

I take a seat next to a flower-box—
an impressionist painting against a bright cerulean wall.
Above, the ivory windows
lead me into centuries of famished love.

So, here we are—
with empty laps
and vacant looks,
accompanied by chairs in attendance.

Warmed by the smell of fresh croissants
and the swirling of autumn leaves—
doodling in empty streets, etching glass walls
rising between us and ceased music.

Winter approaches, grey and chilled.
Conference of black umbrellas in the cemetery:
in a sombre conversation with the dead.
Listen hard to the interstices of the cobblestones—

it is not one sided.
I reach for my coat pocket
to rummage for hope.
Maybe resurrection.

BACK FROM WORK

It used to be a tram stop. The bench and partial awning remain to contemplate the glistening tracks, their last rites forgotten.

This footpath has a secondary purpose. Nocturnal homes for some. Existential homes on their backs. A man walks by crunching toasted peanuts.

The city has many crossroads. The four corners—each hoard a throng. Before we are released in a swarm to swim over. Many will pass each other again.

Fresh puddles tell me it must have rained. Trees, skyscrapers, and tatter-skies bloom in them.
They will again become cloud someday.

Reminds me of Wislawa's 'Water'. What a beautiful poem!
Even in translation. I do not know Polish.
But water like music has no language.

My house is sixteen kilometres away. I will voyage through a flux of metro, buses, and autos. And safeguard a lunchbox and a briefcase. We will not mind the smell of our sweat.

I have a book. I am on page 78. If I stand and I am squashed by fellow travellers, then the story has to wait. Else, I will live briefly in a Colombian village.

This year the winter is short; a couple of weeks. Warm clothes and mothballs are in my grandfather's trunk. Winter may stop visiting our city, some say!

Grown-ups work in an office! I ring the doorbell. I hear two little boys shout in joy. My back hurts, but this is a homecoming ritual. I pick up the little one.

She brings me some tea. With relief we sense our days went well. The next ten minutes are a day within a day. We will be together—though mostly quiet.

BLUE BOAT

The blue boat is not a boat after all.
It floats somewhere in my eyes and
in surrounding spaces, and sways
in the choppy landscape of my mind.

The blue boat has a blue nature,
not of colours and not of thoughts,
but how it sinks with dense heaviness
through the ribcage till it finds

a place that is still and filled with silence.
It never dries, it does not speak,
like I said it is not a boat and it is not blue.
Most of the times it has no medium

and I don't know what it carries inside.
When night comes it turns dark
and stays awake like condensed life.
It lights mud lamps along its edges

and lives on. This is when
stories and dreams are born in its cradle,
and the blue boat sings alone.
At dawn it shines and becomes white light,

pale blue is only a memory, a thin wash.
It is built new and it is ready to sail
on waves of joy and light.
The blue boat sets sail to meet the sun.

SOME NIGHTS

Some nights what a poem can only be
is to hold you tenderly
through the night and cry;
draw you closer and hold you gently,
and muffle its tears
in the lavender expanse of your bosom.
O' my beloved, to cry in your arms,
the night carries away my love,
I can no more bear
holding you tenderly, tenderly near—
is all what a poem can be.

I COME FOR MYSELF

I pass through many hands before
I am returned to myself. I step up to receive
with one last push of strength and pride,
my sad yellow eyes drained of youth's sparkle

and deep folds of skin
that weigh down heavily on my smile
into half-finished joy, and a string of forgetting.
I speak calmly, 'I have come for myself.'

Now I start to sense—how I was built and broken,
the geometry of sharp edges
and stains of blood and sweat that dry
and how the flesh rearranges itself.

All these years,
many faces at work and I can't find myself.
The stones grow dense with cold,
suffering in silence under the cold gaze of stars—

The Boatman of Murshidabad

who keep their distance filled with nothingness,
and forget to tell—I shall die at their hands.
I find a glint lost on the dewed grass,
the only one worth seeking,

we are locked in our eyes under a starry sky,
pushing the universe out, beyond its limits,
like children at play,
and the Gods are watching us.

MONSOON EVENING

Evening is a daily affair, carries its burden of grey
and descends in submission and settles
into the soft pulse of earth and flesh.

The day leaves intervals of wonder, and anguish
of crimson strands and orange flares
immersed gently into an ocean of endless dark. A gasp

like a spike at the end of a laboured whisper,
extinguished and then alive as a precious leftover
of fragrant breath—

is released into a giant hollow; preserves
our faintest faith. A monsoon song
is born at the thrilling tips of infinite raindrops,

leaps into a dance of splashing death—a torrent of
annihilation in a concrete cradle. In the light we could make
the evening is studded with fireflies.

AZURE SOUL

Blueberry night
cotton-wool moonlight.
Sedative pleasure
of caressing the sky.

Far, and farther,
till the limit I can hear.
Feather footsteps
in forlorn drift, from afar.

O, vagabond symphony!
O, peregrine melancholy!
Snared by this chasm,
I hold tight to my chest.

My azure soul
plagued beyond consolation.

INHERITANCE OF SHAME

Now that I have stripped off my shame,
it is a snake's sloughed skin on the ground.
Impotent, infirm, and hollowed out
by the flesh that left, slithering into virgin life.

Its residence in me of dynastic proportions
and its tentacles so ramified.
It spread into every recess, remote and tangled,
imbued all my existences through time.

But now, how do I stand in new balance?
Denuded in lambent light, purged of deadweight?
Like a winter-tree scrutinized in cold light.
Army of goosebumps raid the landscape.

Whose shame is it, anyway?
Voices of self-reproach grow in strength.
How do I renounce the inheritance of shame?
How do I reduce to part-annulled, alien self?

The sloughed skin is vanishing fast
into the elements. Only to form again and again
as incidental shames and people's scars.
History's child carries earth's burden-marks.

TRAIN JOURNEY

Transit of fleeting frames.
The world travels through the window lens.

Tracks run moored to their seeds
like distant, but pressing drum beats.

I am part of the anatomy of a train ride.

Paddy fields stitched in a fresco quilt.
In their arms, quaint hamlets in irenic sleep.

Transmission wires girdle the sky.
They sag in the middle, and then move apart.

Distance tarries. Proximity swishes.
We will all alight at our stations, predestined.

Meanwhile, morning swims in through the ground.
First, I sense the unseen artist at work.
Cadence of plods and splashes churn soft earth.

Then the fields float up as mirror lakes.
Amidst his handiwork of paddy shoots
I see him astride his plough.

I wonder at the journey of my fellow passengers.

The girl beside me wears a lost smile,
akin to the flaking, reminiscing clouds outside.
She smells like a new bride.

We are on the way to see her Ma and Pa again.
In life, we conserve capsules of past lives,
to visit, and revisit, and grow back into old skins.

Right now, every moment is growing larger
and larger to fill our past, and bring it here.

Two little boys made of clay, shiny and naked,
chase a rooster to make it fly.

The rooster teaches them a trick to survive.
So, they won't melt back into the earth in a hurry.

STRANGE TIMES

Strange are these times—
an ant is sent to the gallows
for eating a whale and defrauding the ocean.

The milkman screams in fright
and cows cackle in wicked delight
for the milk has soured in poisoned udders.

From behind the mirror
a peek-a-boo of horror.
Street dogs in terror whine, looking into puddles after
    rain.

Strange are these times—
we breathe fire into shadows so that they swell
and gobble us in an ashen furnace.

Madhu Kailas

A man paralysed by shock climbs hurriedly into the sky.
Clouds draw claws and swoop in fiendishly
to tear off tender buds still in dreamy, tight knots.

Mistrust of flowers with suspect pollen.
Contamination takes the living and the dead.
Canker sores sprout in poets' balderdash.

Stranger times shall beget.
Colder hearts to walk a warmer planet.
We will live to be ancient in spite of dead grains and no
    teeth.

Forgetting how to love and how to die.
When the sun weeps blind, we shall see just as fine.
And nothing will seem to be amiss.

DANCE WITH ANCESTORS

You return in spirit and with the vigour of spring,
explode minutely in each pore of Earth's skin.
Miracles of memory, from the Himalayas
to Kanyakumari, transform into golden limbs.

Bodies renewed in clay rise through the ground,
faces flushed with joy swing to an ancient sound.
We know, we know, those bright eyes in mime
are calling out sweetly to find us again in time.

We follow you along the wheel of people's story
and arrive at the point of return to glory.
Deep in the desert the sand swallows us,
we prevail, we meditate, we create a river.

A billion beats, tuned to a dream, encircle a fire
and chant an ascending hymn. We know, we know,
your voices in prayer will turn us into gemstones
and peace-flowers, from the depths of quiescent centuries.

AFRICAN SUN

'Africa':
A soft, essentially inaudible, whisper,
barely brushing lips to claim existence,

an iota of breath gently released—
forms your name sounded in silence
and in infinite echoes.

The first infusion of breath,
the genesis of our species,
the singular mother to endure our birth.

The children of Pangea
for millions of years
have abandoned your shores.

Africa, you swallowed the sun so deep
you turned into green and black gemstones
that decorate your hurt.

Memories alive in many masks
silent and observing without eyes.
Wood in intricate shapes holds the artists' faith.

Africa, your folklore is the apotheosis of wisdom.
Gifted to generations with your mothers' milk,
and scripted in the white pebble eyes of your stone-men.

Yoruba drums beat
in unison with frisking wildebeests
and play a song of vigour and joy in your being.

In God's own garden
you uphold the ancient convention
of killing without malice, killing without excess.

Look, the sun is a golden veil.
Your honour marches to its own invincible lilt.
Your honour marches to its own invincible lilt.

Madhu Kailas

SEA OF TEARS

A giant wet blanket over the earth
is what I feel waking up.
Everything is dank and weepy. A sense of loss
in your visit and your farewell—a chronicle of our fate.
Retold in absence, in the depth of our sleep.
You touch raw fibres of joy and grief,
of one life, broken in pieces and countless killed
by hands of hatred, screaming shrill.
In our dreams perhaps we cried,
for the little feet running through the Aleppo streets,
we failed and after you had left,
our eyes were still dry.
To the living world we bring back
a sea of tears in a watertight chest,
to wash our blood-spattered body.

WINTER'S PRAYER

Father, winter is here again—
like a mammoth charcoal moth
hovering and hovering, sprinkling minute motes
from wings settling in shivers.

Arid and flaking open my skin,
a faint red streak
speaks from the middle of my parched lips
winter's prayer in split discomfort.

The dust has been set free from the monsoon's bind,
and the withering charms of spring,
long, stale, and fetid. My hands are full
of another year's bounty.

How they rise in swirls
through my creaking spine, blowing away
sediments of time. Unfurling my dusty retinas.
Bits of earth lodge in the mosaic of my heart.

Father, my heart longs to be earthed.
How can I return home to you
with your gift, our burden of love?
I am still your little boy scared of dance-dust.

Give me strength so that one day
I, too, can become the seasons. But, for now—
swathe me in a loving cloth
of familiar smells and calm textures.

And plant me in a haven.
To live here. Even in winter, without leaves
and in melancholy, ambient with stony sun beams.
Forgetting warmth.

My heart tells me:
Let winter not be so lonely, so removed
that you no longer hear your voice, feel my joy.
That we can no longer suffer our company.

The Boatman of Murshidabad

So, I trudge through my sleep
with pain-knots in my knees, and silence in my keep
along your empty streets
strewn with shadows, stones, and earthly prayers.

PURPLE CORD

We are born with heat transmitted to us
to endure a lifetime with warmth,
if only we understood that we were not built
to be cold and merciless.
That purple cord of infinite strength
has annihilated all wars
and wrested love from stone-hearts.
In dust and rubble life rises again,
and again, a child seeks
its mother's breasts with immortal faith.

LATER ON

Later on, we learn to love in a new way
like the old man who peers
into the pistil of a red hibiscus and is lost
in a fusion of wonder and toothless smiles.

Later on, we get to dismantle and forsake
the keepsakes and trifles of a magnificent facade
rippling in a lake of illusion
that opens its heart lovingly to let us go.

Later on, we remember the blank spaces
in our lives mixed with vibrant memories that don't
    belong to us
at the confluence of pilgrims
paying homage to our sacrifice.

Madhu Kailas

Later on, we meet in transparent light
that accentuates our golden nakedness
and seats us inside each other
as comforting visitors to our silence.

MY JOYS
(To: Kolkata)

My joys,
scattered in the streets of your heart,
littered in the shades and siestas of your reverie.

Crowned by the craggy hands of workers
in loincloths, marching out of tarpaulin huts.
Sun and sweat glistening on their skins.

My joys,
being built on your imperial past,
alongside colonial colonnades, dead fountains, and stoic
    busts.

Ripened by cloying summer mangoes,
whetted by the scales and blood of fish,
brewed by your teeming people and your din.

Madhu Kailas

My joys,
loved in your language,
killed by your hurts, flowering in your gardens.

Housed in your houses. Lived in your bodies.
Rushed in your commerce. Wept in your romance.
Conceived in your womb for hundreds of years.

My joys,
cooed in your pigeons, cawed in your ravens,
found in your parks, spoken in whispers of derelict
    benches.

Travelling in wistful trams skirting the Maidan.
Hosted by surreal sunsets of Prinsep Ghat.
Held in the fragile hands of new lovers.

My joys, drowned in your many lakes,
like giant teardrops fallen from the heavens.
My joys, ripple as white clouds across their bosom.

KEYS MADE OF SUNSHINE

A child grows up and learns to listen to silence,
learns to love, and to wait for music.
I search for a lover who has turned blind
and waits patiently through many lives.

You put your hands on my chest.
An explorer's map unfolds with crinkles.
A lock rattles and I go looking for keys made of
    sunshine—
like a happy child.

I am puzzled, I look up at you anxiously,
and you say gently,
'Sleep, my dear, you have forgotten
how to cry.'

Madhu Kailas

SHADOWS ARE BORN OUT OF LIGHT

It is in quiet moments that I see
shadows are born out of light.
How playful with shades and darkness
like courtship in fairy tales,
overlap and intercourse of our souls
without touching our lives.

High up in the tower
the prince and the princess
become lonely pearls of love
and slide down the mountain slopes.

It is in quiet moments that I see
how we try to become gods.
Artisans gild our legs in gold
to hide the mortal flesh and its debilitation.
How fragile we are as mud dissolves in water
and wings of wax drip on to the floor.

The earth has a beautiful body that is finite—
it stopped growing long ago.
Our infinite conceit grows as 'ghost of history'
with no place to go.

A PLANT, A LEAF, A LEAF OF A PLANT, AND I

It has come to this
what started with knowing and naming things.
Charting streets and plotting victories,
maps of youthful energies in urgent print.

I speak to a plant on the windowsill,
attention and kindness extend my will.
A new friend arrives with downy grace,
I lean into the motion of wings that have come to rest.
Space remembers long after it is shuffled,
and we forget.

A green leaf, out of focus, is bloated inside my eyes.
It melts at the edges and flows outwards,
a leaf grows into my whole world,
the rest falls apart, stands aside.
In peace, in place—
a plant, a leaf, a leaf of a plant, and I.

We keep company watched by a wooden frame,
we become a picture, hemmed in an instant.
We are an instant in a window, in the middle of passage.
Life is an instant we hold tenuously together.

THE FLUTE PLAYER

Lately we have not spoken about
how you will play the flute, and how I will listen.
Your breath as music enters my still heart
bursting like a universe of joy, spreading ripples.

There are things I like to tell to emptiness
like giving birth to secrets.
The sound of your name rolling
in the intimacy of my tongue, my breath.

The long-forgotten story of the deer
that opens its almond-eyes and spills baby-suns.
Your cradle—the betel-leaf space of your lap
built by your immense ivory thighs.

It is late in the day, and lately I can hear you play
the flute in the wilderness. Somewhere you have found
    yourself,

and somewhere else I found you too.
You move between mountains like voluptuous shades

and ride through the valleys to the edge
where the sun sprouts again in warm, golden scape.
It is late in the day and I sit in silence,
lately I can hear you play the flute in the distance.

ACKNOWLEDGEMENTS

I would like to thank David Davidar, Aienla Ozukum, Isha Banerji, and other members of the team at Aleph Book Company for making this book happen. It was fantastic to have David's and Aienla's guidance on selecting the poems for this; moreover, their impeccable attention to detail and editorial matters was invaluable. Working with them on the editorial process has been a great learning experience for me.

I published my first book of poems few years ago. In the years since then, I have published poems in various poetry journals around the world. Each time an editor picked a poem for publication it was an immeasurable encouragement for me. These have kept me going, and of course, the undeniable and unexplainable draw toward poetry. I would like to thank Yashodhara Mishra and A. J. Thomas of *Indian Literature*, Jessica Issacs and Rayshell Clapper of *Dragon Poet Review*, Patricia Oxley of *Acumen*, Nick Siefert of *The Amistad*, Dave Essinger of *Slippery Elm*, Joe Baumann of *Gateway Review*, and the teams at *Marathon Literary Review* and *New Mexico Review* for their kindness.

My deep gratitude to all fellow poets and poetry lovers with whom I interact; we hold each other's work gently for the poems to breathe. I am indebted to my wife, Madhumita, and our two boys for their understanding and their patience with my adventures with poetry.

⁂

Some of the poems in the book first appeared in the following journals. A few of them have been edited for this volume.
Notes on Drought—*Indian Literature*, March–April 2015
Copper Mine—*Dragon Poet Review*, Winter 2014
Poetry for Tomorrow—*Dragon Poet Review*, Winter 2014
The Boatman of Murshidabad—*Indian Literature*, March–April 2015
Shakuntala's Plea—*Indian Literature*, March–April 2015
Winter's Prayer—*New Mexico Review*, Fall 2016
Sidewalk Café—*Marathon Literary Review*, August 2017
A Plant, a Leaf, a Leaf of a Plant, and I—*Slippery Elm*, May 2019
Monsoon Evening—*Indian Literature*, September–October 2019

Music of Our Species—*Indian Literature*, September–October 2019
Statue's Poem—*Indian Literature*, September–October 2019
How Strong You had to Be—From a Miner's Son—*Indian Literature*, September–October 2019
The Day a Song Dared to Soar—*The Amistad*, April 2020
Born Again as a Cherry Tree—*Dragon Poet Review*, Fall 2019
Darjeeling—*LangLit*, 2017
Love Grows—*Indian Literature*, March–April 2015
Transparent Men—*Poets Corner Anthology*, 2014–15
My Joys—*Poets Corner Anthology*, 2014–15
The Flute Player—*Acumen*, Jan 2021

INDEX OF FIRST LINES

A child grows up and learns to listen to silence,	92
A deserted station and a long wait.	41
'Africa':	81
A giant wet blanket over the earth	83
A sweep of your eyelashes	50
A thin layer—sparkle of glass,	49
Beyond remembrance, you are so distant,	18
Blueberry night	72
Butterflies descend. Twin yellow leaves float;	59
Evening is a daily affair, carries its burden of grey	71
Father, winter is here again—	84
Hollowed earth—	3
How strong you were, now I know	52
I hear your demure flute	25
I kneel down and bend forward awkwardly	28
I pass through many hands before	69
I wait for you	62
In a small village, by the sea,	16
In an apartment	5

It has come to this	95
It is in quiet moments that I see	93
It used to be a tram stop.	64
Lately we have not spoken about	97
Later on, we learn to love in a new way	88
Lips chiselled into an enduring smile,	34
Long shadows in the snow.	46
Longing arrives	55
Love grows	30
Mother, you sent me into this world	60
My joys,	90
Now that I have stripped off my shame,	73
Now the hills call (again), rising into the sky	43
Once a man	14
Open skies pouring stars…	8
Our explorer friends	21
Some nights what a poem can only be	68
Strange are these times—	78
The blue boat is not a boat after all.	66
The boat holds still its inverted self	36
The day the travellers returned	1

The earth nibbles on traces of desiccated grass and polishes itself.	12
The forest has a song that plays	57
The glistening blade of the ocean	45
The rock has a womb of faith,	23
Transit of fleeting frames.	75
We are born with heat transmitted to us	87
Yesterday is reduced to a midget box	47
You are so quiet I can almost listen to *you beating*.	10
You leave for the mountains	39
You return in spirit and with the vigour of spring,	80

ABOUT THE POET

Madhu Kailas is the pen name of Kingshuk Basu. He is a native of Kolkata and has lived in various places in India and the USA. He is the author of *The Birds Fly in Silence*. His poems have been published in journals like the *Gateway Review, Marathon Literary Review, Literary Voyage, Indian Literature, The Amistad, Slippery Elm, Dragon Poet Review, New Mexico Review, Acumen,* and *Langlit*. He studied Electrical Engineering at the Indian Institute of Technology, Kanpur, and Business Management at Michigan State University. He lives with his wife and children in Mumbai.